HARLEM'S TALE OF HOPE

By HARLEM HOLIDAY

Inspired by the story of William 'Donnell' Porter
May 20, 1977 – January 28, 1990

Harlem Holiday
New York, New York

HARLEM'S TALE OF HOPE
By HARLEM HOLIDAY
New York, New York

Copyright © 2023 Harlem Holiday

Without limiting the rights under copyright reserved above, no part of this publication may be reproduced, stored in or introduced into a retrieval system, or transmitted in any form or by any means (electronic, mechanical, photocopying, recording or otherwise), without the prior written permission of the copyright owner.

Illustrations by Stephanie Hider
Foreword by Patricia Porter
Cover Design by Najdan Mancic

Scanning, uploading, and distributing this book via the Internet or any other means without the publisher's permission is illegal and punishable by law. Please purchase only authorized electronic editions and do not participate in or encourage electronic piracy of copyright materials. Your support of the author's rights is appreciated.

Paperback ISBN: 978-1-7375699-2-3
Hardcover ISBN: 978-1-7375699-3-0
Printed in the United States of America

1st Edition
Harlem Westside Publishing LLC
New York, NY 10026
www.harlemwestsidepublishing.com

McGruff the Crime Dog® and "Take A Bite Out Of Crime®" are registered marks of the National Crime Prevention Council.

In loving memory of

WILLIAM DONNELL PORTER

Whose laughter and light continue to inspire us, and whose legacy shines as a beacon of hope. This book is dedicated to all the children of color who have gone missing, their stories often unheard, their faces unseen.

In 2022, 214,582 persons of color were reported missing. Of that group, 153,374 were under the age of 18, as reported by the Black and Missing Foundation, Inc. (BAMFI). Yet, missing minority children are grossly underreported in the news.

We dedicate this book to raise awareness, to shine a light on these missing voices, and to inspire a safer, more compassionate world for all children, everywhere.

May we never forget, may we always strive to protect, and may hope guide us towards a brighter future.

Released during National Child Safety and Protection Month,

November 2023.

FOREWORD

My Open Heart To Harlem,

I want to express my deepest gratitude and extend a special thank you to the remarkable author, Harlem Holiday, for her unwavering dedication to preserving the memory of my beloved younger brother, William Donnell Porter. Through her resolute storytelling, she has breathed life into his story, transforming it into a cautionary tale that serves as a beacon of awareness for our children, guiding them through the concealed dangers that lurk beyond the safety of their homes.

To all those who have remained steadfast in their loyalty to The Porter Family over the years, I am profoundly thankful. Though the passage of time may suggest healing, the pain of Donnell's tragic departure from this world remains as fresh as ever. There is no semblance of normalcy in the manner in which he was taken from us.

Throughout these years, many have spoken of my strength, but today, I want to acknowledge that this strength has been fortified by each one of you who has allowed me to express it openly and authentically, free from judgment. Your unwavering support, whether through small gestures or monumental efforts, has sustained me in ways words cannot fully convey. In the midst of loss, I have also found gain – the unwavering hearts of Harlem, standing by me, unyielding in their love. To each and every one of you, I extend my profound love and gratitude.

Surviving these years has been an arduous journey, but it is knowing that the embrace of Harlem's love has held me close to its heart that has enabled me to persevere. Today, we celebrate not only ourselves but also the collective strength and resilience of Harlem. It is through this unity that Harlem heals, and Harlem endures.

Love,

Patricia Porter

In the vibrant city of Harlem,
where dreams are alive,
Lived a young boy named Donnell,
with hopes that would thrive.

Bright and energetic,
he walked to school each day,
Little did he know,
danger would come his way.

In 1989, a stranger crossed his path,
With intentions so dark, it filled the community with wrath.

Donnell was taken,
his family left in despair,
A search began, a plea
for their beloved
to be back in their care.

Harlem's streets,
where families roam,
Donnell went missing,
far from home.

His folks, so sad,
with hearts in pain,
They searched for him,
but all in vain.

His laughter unheard,
his presence unseen,
A nightmare they lived in,
a constant dream.

Donnell's Birthday Celebration, May 20th

Amidst the turmoil,
McGruff the Crime Dog appeared,
To PS 92, where children gathered
and cheered.

"Trust your instincts,"
McGruff wisely proclaimed,
If something feels off, it's not just a game.

"Stranger danger," he warned,
with a concerned frown,
Never go with unknown faces,
stay safe in your town.

"Stay in groups,"
McGruff advised with a smile,
For together, in unity,
we can conquer any trial.

Know the safe places, where help can be sought,
From trusted neighbors' homes to police stations, lessons to be taught.

NO!

Be aware of surroundings,
avoid distractions at hand,
Look up, not down,
and take charge of the land.

"Speak up," he encouraged,
"with a firm and loud 'NO'!"
For children have the power,
and their voices will glow.

The children of PS 92
listened with wide eyes,
Absorbing the knowledge,
their spirits began to rise.

McGruff's teachings,
Donnell's story intertwined,
A lasting legacy of resilience,
forever in their minds.

Patricia, with resolve,
continued her quest,
To keep Donnell's memory alive,
to give it its best.

Through the pain and the sorrow,
she fought for the cause,
To prevent other families
from facing such loss.

Patricia, Donnell's sister,
a beacon of strength,
Advocated tirelessly,
going to any length.

She raised awareness,
spoke at schools and events,
To avoid such tragedies,
her voice was heaven-sent.

Adam Clayton Powell Jr.
Blvd

William Donnell Porter
Way

W 132 St

PS 92 honored Donnell,
a symbol of light,
A memorial plaque,
shining precious and bright.

A reminder to keep their
community safe and sound,
In Donnell's name,
unity was found.

William 'Donnell' Porter
1977-1990

Through the passing years,
PS 92 stood tall,
Educating children,
sharing safety for all.

McGruff made his visits,
reinforcing the creed,
That safety and vigilance
were the tools they would need.

Donnell's tale became a powerful guide,
Resilience and caution standing side by side.

A community united, protecting each child,
Building a haven where dreams could run wild.

Harlem's children learned,
with hearts full of grace,
To trust their instincts,
making safety a chase.

Together they stood,
protecting one another,
Building a place
where kindness hovers.

Donnell's memory lived on,
a beacon so bright,
A reminder that safety
is a collective fight.

Through Patricia's love
and the community's embrace,
A difference was made,
spreading hope's embrace.

So remember, dear children,
as you walk through your day,
In Harlem or beyond,
wherever you may stray,

Stay vigilant, speak up,
and hold safety tight,
For in unity and courage,
we find our greatest light.

The tale of Harlem's hope,
Donnell's legacy so grand,
A story of resilience,
a call to take a stand.

In every child's heart,
a spark will forever burn,
To protect and inspire,
for there's much more to learn.

The End

MEET HARLEM HOLIDAY: A LITERARY LUMINARY AND CHANGEMAKER

Harlem Holiday, a bestselling author, weaves enchanting tales that transport readers to magical realms and spark their imaginations. Rooted in Harlem, her unwavering commitment to positive change shines through her words and actions. As a prominent figure in literature, her captivating stories and advocacy inspire transformation. Watch for her upcoming releases and be enchanted by her literary magic. Harlem Holiday—a name synonymous with captivating stories and making the world better, one word at a time.

FOLLOW HARLEM HOLIDAY

instagram

facebook

twitter